Presented to the Saltcreek TWP Library by the
Saltcreek PTO.   1975

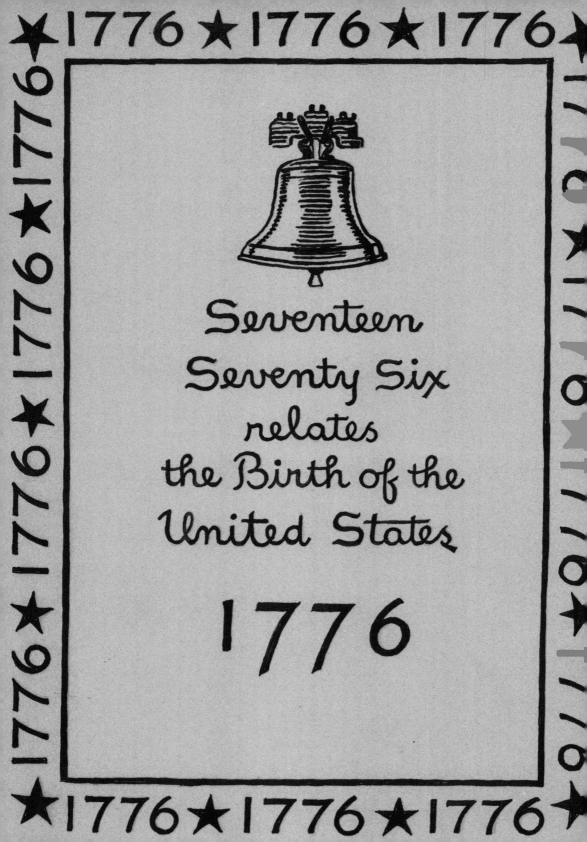

Seventeen
Seventy Six
relates
the Birth of the
United States

1776

YEAR OF
INDEPENDENCE
1776

by Genevieve Foster

Charles Scribner's Sons   *New York*

3 5 7 9 11 13 15 17 19 **RD/C** 20 18 16 14 12 10 8 6 4 2
Printed in the United States of America
SBN-684-82063-3
Library of Congress Catalog Card Number 75-106531

CONTENTS

Washington

Part One

THE
AMERICAN
COLONIES

Jefferson

Franklin

George III

THE YEAR WAS 1776. It was the fourth of July. At an early hour, while the morning was still cool, delegates from the thirteen American colonies were entering the red brick State House in Philadelphia for a meeting of Congress.

Thomas Jefferson, from Virginia, was in a most unhappy frame of mind. Yesterday had been a miserable day. He had had to sit and listen while the delegates tore apart and criticized an announcement he had been asked to write. This was a declaration to be sent to the King of England, telling

1776

him that the colonies had decided to be "free and independent states" and why they had made this decision. Thomas Jefferson had worked hard on it for two weeks. He had done his best. What fault would they find with it today? he wondered. Entering the East Room, he took his seat at one of the small tables facing a low platform.

At the same table were two other members of the committee appointed by Congress to draw up this declaration. One of them was Benjamin Franklin of Philadelphia, the oldest and most famous of the delegates. The old gentleman tried again, as he had the day before, to cheer up the downhearted young author with a friendly word or an amusing story.

John Adams, the other person at the table, was a man who never feared to speak his mind. He had insisted that Thomas Jefferson should write the declaration. He had no doubt that it would be approved today.

The buzz of conversation and the noisy scraping of chairs filled the room, until there came the sharp rap of a gavel. The meeting was being called to order by the President, John Hancock of Boston, a handsome man richly dressed in a red velvet suit trimmed in gold braid and buttons.

The Secretary rose and read the important paper from beginning to end. Most of the words were just as Thomas Jefferson had written them. The declaration was approved, ready to be copied on parchment and signed.

John Hancock, the first to sign it, wrote his name very big and black. "There," said he, "King George will have no trouble reading that without his spectacles."

Benjamin Franklin is said to have remarked later, after signing his name, "Now, my friends, we must all hang together or we will hang separately." Everyone knew what he meant. Hanging was the punishment for traitors. Every signer of that declaration would be called a traitor by the king. They would have to hang together firmly to win their freedom. Would they be able to?

Why had they broken away from England in the first place? Did all the people want to? Why didn't George Washington sign the Declaration of Independence?

These questions are answered in this story which begins in 1760, the year that George III became King of England.

The Thirteen Colonies

THIS IS KING GEORGE III as he looked in 1760 when he had just been crowned in Westminster Abbey and had first heard his joyful people cheering, "God Save the King!"

The English people were indeed joyful because here, at last, they had a king who had been born in England instead of in Germany. It was not long before they discovered that

1760

George III differed in more ways than one from his German ancestors. Those two kings, George I and George II, had cared so little about England they had been quite willing to let Parliament rule the country. Not so George III. He was a stubborn young man, set on being the kind of king whose word counted for something in the government. Very soon he was in deep trouble with his American colonies over taxes.

The Stamp Act was the tax law that caused the greatest uproar. In 1765 small stamps were sent to the colonies which had to be bought and stuck on a number of things, such as newspapers, almanacs, playing cards, and legal documents. No sooner had the stamps arrived than the people rebelled. Angry meetings were held in all of the colonies.

In Boston, Massachusetts, the leading rebel was Samuel Adams, John Adams's cousin. He told a meeting of shipowners

1765

and merchants that they did not have to pay the tax. John Adams agreed with him. Both said that the colonists should not have to pay the stamp tax because they had not consented to pay it. And, according to law, "No Englishman could be made to pay any tax to which he had not given his consent."

Patrick Henry, a Virginia lawyer, said the same thing at a meeting of planters in Williamsburg, Virginia. George Washington was there and heard the fiery orator remind George III of another king of England who had had his head chopped off for having pushed the people too far.

Impatient, hot-headed people calling themselves "Sons of Liberty" destroyed the stamps, insulted and attacked the king's officers who had the stamps for sale. So the Stamp Act had to be repealed, but it was followed by a new tax law.

New taxes were placed on many things the colonists had to buy from England, such as glass, paper, paints, china, and tea. They refused to buy them. Then the English merchants complained, and these taxes also were repealed. But not entirely!

George III was too stubborn for that. Just to prove that he had a perfect right to tax the colonies, he had the tax left on one thing. That one thing was TEA.

IN DECEMBER, 1773, three English tea ships were anchored in Boston Harbor. The harbor master refused to accept the tea. The captains refused to sail away until the tea was unloaded. So there the tea stood, until Samuel Adams had an idea for what was later to be called the "Boston Tea Party."

Late one afternoon wild war whoops were heard. Racing toward the harbor went a band of young men dressed like

14

1773

Indians. They boarded the ships, smashed open the Chinese tea chests, and dumped them into the water.

King George turned red with rage at this rebellious act. He ordered Boston Harbor closed and sent four regiments of soldiers to control the people. The Boston people jeered at the soldiers, called them "Redcoats" and "Lobsterbacks" because of their red uniforms. The soldiers jeered back at the people, calling them the scornful nickname of "Yankee."

When the Virginians heard what had been happening in Boston, they thought the time had come for men from all of the colonies to meet and talk together. Plans were made for a Continental Congress to be held in Philadelphia. Early in September, 1774, delegates from north and south were traveling on horseback or in coaches along the dusty roads leading to Philadelphia. All were curious to see what the strangers from the other colonies were like. Many were shocked to hear it whispered that the Boston delegates wanted to be "free from England." None of the other delegates could imagine being anything but loyal to their king. Therefore, as "His Majesty's loyal Subjects," they wrote to George III, asking for their rights as Englishmen. Then they went home, planning to meet again in May, when they hoped to have an answer from the

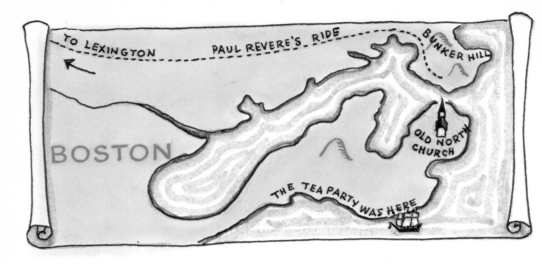

king. Winter passed. Spring came. Still there was no answer.

"It is useless to wait any longer," said Patrick Henry at a meeting in Virginia. "We must fight for our rights. I know not what others may choose, but for me . . .

GIVE ME LIBERTY OR GIVE ME DEATH."

The Virginia planters now began to train companies of soldiers, with George Washington in command.

Massachusetts farmers calling themselves "minutemen" stood ready to fight at a minute's notice. They had bullets, gunpowder, and other supplies stored in the town of Concord.

One evening in April, 1775, the people of Boston learned that the British soldiers were going to Concord to seize whatever was stored there. A lookout was stationed in the steeple of Old North Church to signal with his lantern when he saw the soldiers starting. Down below two men on horseback were

1775

watching. One of them was Paul Revere. Suddenly, at midnight, the lantern flashed and they were off, riding through farms and villages crying, "To arms! To arms! The British are coming! The Redcoats are on the way!"

Early next morning, in the chill gray dawn, fifty minutemen were gathered on the village green at Lexington, facing a company of British soldiers.

"Disperse, ye rebels!" shouted the British commander.

Shots were fired. No one knows who fired first. But with that first shot on the green at Lexington, the American Revolution began. It was the morning of April 19, 1775.

At Concord more minutemen waited at a small wooden bridge to drive off the British soldiers, who then left on a swift march back to Boston. By this time, all along the way, angry farmers were crouched behind the low stone walls with their muskets ready to fire. Soon, instead of marching, the Redcoats were running for their lives. The farmers were so proud of this first skirmish with the British they were even proud to be called Yankee. Soon they were singing the old British song "Yankee Doodle," and it became the marching tune of the American Revolution.

On May 25, three British generals and more British troops arrived in Boston Harbor. Minutemen and farmers put up a good fight against them at the Battle of Bunker Hill, but by the end of June the British had moved into Boston. And the makeshift army of Americans was camped on the hills surrounding the city.

John Adams heard this news in Philadelphia, where the Second Continental Congress had been meeting since May.

GEORGE WASHINGTON went to the Second Continental Congress in his military uniform, showing that he was ready for action.

John Adams saw him and spoke up at once. "I propose," he said, "that this Congress adopt the army outside Boston and appoint the gentleman from Virginia as commander."

They could hardly be called an army, those minutemen and farmers that George Washington found gathered on the hills outside of Boston. But he began to train them. There was no way, as yet, for him to drive the British out of Boston because he had no cannon.

In March, 1776, when a number of cannon were delivered to Washington, the British general saw them through his spyglass and sent word not to fire. He had decided to leave Boston. As soon as Washington saw the British sail away, he marched his small, ragged army down to New York, believing that New York was the next city which the British would try to capture.

That is why George Washington did not sign the Declara-

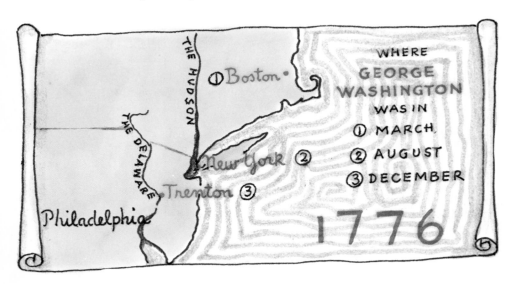

THE HUDSON
① Boston
THE DELAWARE
New York ②
Trenton ③
Philadelphia

WHERE
GEORGE
WASHINGTON
WAS IN
① MARCH
② AUGUST
③ DECEMBER
1776

tion of Independence. On July 4, 1776, he was in New York City with his soldiers, fighting to make that brave declaration come true. He had it read aloud to the soldiers when a copy reached him in August. By then the British had him surrounded. He barely managed to get his army across the Hudson River into New Jersey.

German soldiers had been hired by the British and brought to America to fight. Under the command of the English General Cornwallis, they chased Washington and his men down through New Jersey. By Christmas Eve they had reached Trenton, on the Delaware River. Washington crossed the icy river into Pennsylvania. Cornwallis remained in Trenton.

Christmas night came. The German soldiers were still celebrating the holiday when all of a sudden they were surrounded and captured. Washington was there and two hundred of his men, covered with sleet and snow. They had come back across the Delaware to make this surprise attack.

So the famous year 1776 ended. The rest of the winter Washington spent in camp near Morristown, New Jersey. Those were miserable months. The soldiers got almost no food or clothing from Congress, and no pay. Washington often paid them with his own money to keep them from deserting.

1776

IN PHILADELPHIA, not far away from the State House where Congress was meeting, was the small brick house of Mrs. Betsy Ross. In the summer of 1777 she was making the first American flags, according to a design that Congress had approved on July 14. George Washington may have talked to Betsy Ross about it, for he was then in Philadelphia.

General Washington had come to Philadelphia to talk to Congress about getting more supplies and pay for his ragged soldiers. But it was hard to see what could be done. Congress had no money and no way of making the colonies pay to support the war unless they wanted to. And in every colony there were many Loyalists, who would pay nothing to support this war against the king.

By September 26, 1777, the British had captured Philadelphia. And the members of Congress had scrambled their papers together and fled to another Pennsylvania town.

Benjamin Franklin, Philadelphia's most famous citizen, was not there when the British moved in. He was in France. As soon as the Declaration of Independence had been signed, Congress had sent him to try to persuade the French to join the Americans in the war against England. He had sailed from Philadelphia in November, 1776, taking his two grandsons with him. It was a long, cold, rough crossing. Hardly had the ship reached the French harbor when the news that Benjamin Franklin was there traveled ahead of him to Paris. The great Dr. Franklin, famous all over Europe for his experiments with electricity, had arrived in France!

THE KING OF FRANCE at this time was Louis XVI. He was a good, honest, clumsy fellow who had never wanted to be king. Before he was crowned, he was happy to spend his days making locks. He had now given that up and was trying to do the best he could at being king. He and his very gay, fun-loving queen, Marie Antoinette, lived in a gorgeous palace at Versailles, about ten miles from Paris. This had been built by Louis XVI's great-great-great grandfather, Louis XIV, a great warrior as well as a great statesman.

Louis XVI was no warrior. He did not want to join in this war against England. Another war meant more taxes for the poor people of France, who already complained about having too many taxes to pay. But his ministers talked so fast and gave so many reasons for France to sign a treaty with the American colonies that Louis XVI finally gave in and wrote the large capital L that was his signature. And on February 6, 1778, Benjamin Franklin also signed this famous treaty.

24

A few weeks later Franklin was presented to the king as a representative of the new nation, which the French then spoke of as the "United Provinces of America."

1778

THAT WAS A JOYFUL DAY when the good news from France reached the American army camp at Valley Forge. No one there could have been happier than Lafayette, the young French *marquis* who had been serving under General Washington for almost a year. The king had forbidden Lafayette to leave France, so he slipped away in disguise, his heart set on joining the glorious fight for liberty. Now that

Lafayette

his country had joined the war, Lafayette went home as a hero.

Louis XVI invited him to Versailles and asked him about General Washington. Marie Antoinette invited him to dance with her at a court ball. Lafayette even hoped that he might be given command of the army that was to be sent to America. He was too young for that he was told, but he could go on ahead to announce to General Washington that the French army would soon be on its way.

In the late summer of 1780 the French army arrived. Then, soon after Washington had met the French commander, he made a shocking discovery. He found that Benedict Arnold, one of his most trusted officers, was a traitor. Arnold had been plotting to turn the American fort at West Point over to the British general in New York. Six months later Washington heard that Benedict Arnold, in command of British troops, was marching through Virginia, laying waste to the plantations. Washington sent Lafayette to Virginia with orders to capture the scoundrel, dead or alive.

Washington himself and the French commander were waiting near New York for the French fleet to arrive so that they could attack the British troops in New York and recapture the city. Meanwhile, the British General Cornwallis, who had

1780

been in South Carolina and Georgia, hurried north into Virginia. He intended to capture Lafayette before Lafayette could capture Benedict Arnold.

"That French boy cannot escape me," Cornwallis boasted. But soon it was Cornwallis himself who could not escape. He was trapped on the peninsula at Yorktown. From then on, one disappointment followed another for that unhappy man.

The British general in New York was supposed to send the British fleet to help him, but before it came, a French fleet came sailing into Chesapeake Bay. Cornwallis was also counting on the general in New York to send him more soldiers. Before they arrived, Washington and the French commander had joined Lafayette. That made about 9,000 American and 6,000 French soldiers outside Yorktown. Inside the town the British soldiers were starving and dying.

On October 19, ten days after the cannon began firing at Yorktown, Cornwallis raised the white flag and surrendered. On that autumn afternoon the British troops in their soiled red uniforms marched slowly out of Yorktown, passing between lines of French and American troops, who stood in respectful silence in obedience to Washington's command.

So on October 19, 1781, the American Revolution ended.

1781

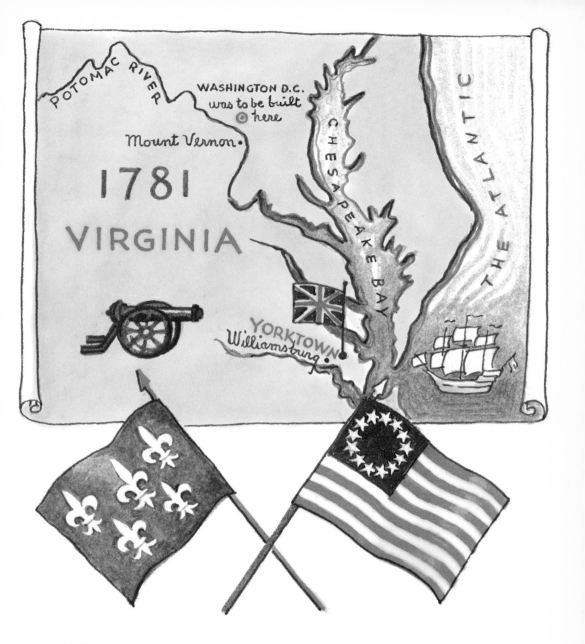

I T WAS TWO MORE YEARS before the Peace Treaty was
signed. Then, in 1783, George III recognized the inde-

pendence of the United States in the House of Lords. He ended a formal speech by saying that he hoped, since they had the same language and the same religion, there would be a lasting friendship between the two nations.

Actually, George III wondered how long this small, weak, newborn nation would survive. What would happen next? Most wars ended by having the victorious military leader seize the power. Would Washington seize the power and make himself king? The person he asked replied that he would not.

"If he does not," the king replied, "George Washington will be the greatest man in the world today."

Washington's soldiers had made this suggestion. They had been so disgusted with the way Congress had mistreated them, they felt that if Washington did not seize the power someone else would.

George Washington was shocked. He begged them not to destroy the freedom they had won. And so because they trusted him, this government by the people would survive. And George Washington, who had been "first in war," was to be "first in peace and first in the hearts of his countrymen"—the first President of the United States.

Voltaire

Part Two

ARTISTS
AND
SCIENTISTS

Montgolfier

Lavoisier

Mozart

THE UNITED STATES OF AMERICA was just seven years old when aviation was born in France. Benjamin Franklin was there and watched with great excitement the first voyage in the air ever taken by man. In November, 1783, he saw two daring young Frenchmen go up in a balloon and ride for twenty minutes over the housetops of Paris.

Before that, three animals—a sheep, a duck, and a rooster—

Montgolfier

had been sent up in a balloon to test what had long been supposed to be the "dangerous upper air." To everyone's amazement they came down alive and quite unharmed. After that, balloons were the great topic of conversation in Paris and Versailles. No one took a more lively interest in the subject than the old scientist Benjamin Franklin. Someone asked him why, of what use were balloons?

"Of what *use* is a new-born baby?" answered Benjamin Franklin. He could see that as surely as a baby grows to be a man, these first balloon experiments would grow into a new way of traveling—by air.

The Montgolfier brothers, Joseph and Stephen, were the inventors of the balloon. They had grown up in a small town in southern France. One day, looking up into the summer sky full of white clouds, the younger brother had said: "I believe if one could capture a cloud in a paper bag, it would carry the bag up and an extra weight as well. But, alas, how does one capture a cloud?"

Then they thought, why not try to make a bag rise by filling it with hot air and smoke? The brothers made several trial balloons and then gave a public demonstration in the marketplace of their hometown. The huge blue paper balloon rose like a thing bewitched and sailed away! The news spread like wildfire. Scientists invited the Montgolfiers to Paris. Louis XVI asked them to bring their balloon to Versailles so that he and the court might see it take off from the palace gardens. The next day Benjamin Franklin wrote a letter to the President of the Royal Society in London, of which he was a member:

"Dear Sir: Enclosed is a copy of the Experiment made yesterday in the Garden of the Palace, which being near my house, I was present. The balloon was larger than that which carried the Sheep etc. Its bottom was open and in the middle of the Opening was a kind of basket in which faggots and sheaves of straw were burnt. When it went over our heads we could see the Fire. . . . One of these Courageous Philosophers did me the honor to call upon me in the evening with Mr. Montgolfier, the Inventor of the Balloon.

"[It is only] a few months since the idea of witches riding through the air on a broomstick, and Philosophers upon a bag of smoke would have appeared equally ridiculous.

"I begin to be almost sorry I was born so soon, since I cannot have the happiness of knowing what will be known a hundred years from now."

O IS THE SYMBOL FOR OXYGEN, the best known symbol used in chemistry. Today we all know that oxygen is part of the air we breathe; that we must have it to live; that without extra oxygen, flying at high altitudes would not be possible. Yet before 1774, no one had ever heard of oxygen.

36

Oxygen

A French scientist, Antoine Lavoisier, invented the name. This drawing shows Lavoisier working with two associates in his laboratory. At the table behind him is his young wife, taking notes. She and her husband were dear friends of Benjamin Franklin while he was in Paris.

Lavoisier did not discover oxygen. This had been done by an older friend of Benjamin Franklin, an Englishman named

Lavoisier

Joseph Priestley. He and a Swedish scientist had discovered this "strange kind of air" at about the same time. In 1774 Mr. Priestley was in Paris. Lavoisier invited him to dinner. Priestley mentioned his discovery, saying that he had found a kind of air in which a candle burned much brighter than in common air. He added, "I have not yet given it any name."

Lavoisier was not satisfied. He wanted to know what process was going on. Why did the nameless air make a candle burn brighter? For thousands of years, men had been breathing air without knowing what happened to it in their lungs. Lavoisier had an idea: Could breathing possibly be a kind of burning? He wanted to find out. He began to test his idea in his laboratory and found that in both breathing and burning, one gas in the air remained unchanged and another was used up. That part of the air that was used up, Lavoisier called oxygen. The unused gas he named nitrogen, giving it the symbol N. The process he discovered in his experiments is one of the most important of all chemical processes: *oxidation*.

Lavoisier continued, with the help of other French scientists, to work out names and symbols that are used in chemistry today, and he also wrote the first textbook in the field. He is often called "the father of modern chemistry."

IT WAS SUNDAY, FEBRUARY 15, 1778. In a hotel room in Paris, a wisp of a Frenchman, eighty-four years old, sat in his bed feverishly writing a letter. He signed it VOLTAIRE, handed it to his secretary, and then turned to a play, called *Irene,* which he was also writing.

Voltaire

He was supposed to be resting. Those were doctor's orders. But rest? Impossible! Rest on his first visit to Paris in twenty years? Rest when there were so many people to see? Three hundred people had come to see him on the day after he arrived from his home in Switzerland.

This Sunday morning, Benjamin Franklin, the illustrious American philosopher, was waiting to be introduced. His grandson was with him. Voltaire greeted them in English and then spoke of America. His old eyes sparkled.

"If I were forty years younger," he said, "I should go and settle in your happy country."

To Voltaire, the United States and its government represented the things he had been writing about and fighting for all his life. Liberty. Equality. Brotherhood. Always he had upheld the rights of the French people against oppression by their overlords and kings. For that he had won the love of the people and the hatred and fear of the nobles and kings. More than once they had had him thrown into prison.

The first time he was twenty-three years old and known as François Marie Arouet. While he was writing in prison, he decided to use the pen name "Voltaire."

The second time he was in prison, he was set free on condition that he would leave France. Then he went to England. After three years he returned, saying how much better the English government was than that of France, especially in regard to taxes. His book on England was burned by the royal executioner, and again Voltaire had to leave France.

"That Voltaire," said one of his enemies, "ought to be locked up where he could get neither pen, ink, nor paper. Such a man is capable of destroying a kingdom."

Voltaire wished only to reform, not to destroy the kingdom of France. But by teaching the French people to think of fighting for their rights, he helped to bring on a bloody revolution in which the king would be beheaded and the kingdom destroyed. This French Revolution began in 1789. Voltaire did not live to see it; he died in May, 1778, in his hotel in Paris.

In March of that year, he had gone to the theatre to see his play *Irene* performed and received a great ovation. As he entered, the audience stood and cheered. The actors crowned him with laurel. Crowds carrying lighted torches walked beside his carriage back to the hotel, singing and dancing. And then they wept as they saw the fragile old man step from the coach, wave to them briefly, and disappear.

THE YOUNG MUSICIAN Wolfgang Mozart was downhearted. His bags were packed. He was leaving France.
It was September, 1778. He had been in Paris six months,
and he had failed to find a wealthy patron. He had to go back
home now to Salzburg, Austria, and face his disappointed
father, his father who had sent him off with such high hopes.

"Off with you to Paris!" his father said. "Take your right-
ful place among those who are truly great."

Mozart's father, who was a violinist, had known from the time Wolfgang was four that he was a genius. With tears of wonder and delight he had come upon the small boy writing a concerto for the clavier. When the boy was five, he wrote a "Minuet in G" and taught himself to play the violin.

In 1762, when Wolfgang was six and his sister Marianna was eleven, their father took his "wonder children" on a grand concert tour, to play before the kings and queens of Europe.

In Vienna, the capital of Austria, they performed for the Empress Maria Theresa. She was so warm and motherly that little Wolfgang jumped into her lap and kissed her many times. He also liked the little Princess Marie Antoinette, who was about his age. One day as they were playing together he slipped and fell, and she helped him up.

"You are good," he said. "Someday I shall marry you!"

The Empress smiled. Plans had already been made for her small daughter to marry the future King of France, Louis XVI.

In 1778 Marie Antoinette had been Queen of France for four years. Mozart had not seen her. His father had written to Vienna for an introduction, but it never came. The concerts Wolfgang had given in Paris had been a disappointment. He could have given music lessons, but that paid very little and meant running all over Paris. That would have left no time for writing music, which was the most important thing in life to him. This he continued to do as long as he lived.

Although Mozart grew poorer and poorer and more miserable, and died when he was only thirty-five, he left the world a wealth of marvelous music. One of the last operas he wrote was the lovely *Magic Flute.*

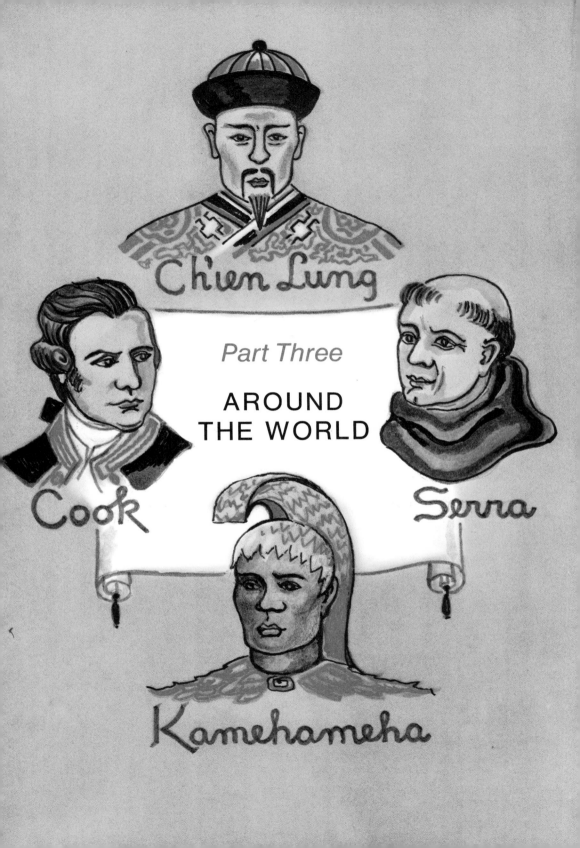

Ch'ien Lung

Cook

Part Three

AROUND
THE WORLD

Serra

Kamehameha

ARCTIC OCEAN

RUS

ATLANTIC
OCEAN

AFRICA

SOUTH
AMERICA

ATLANTIC OCEAN

······ First Voyage of Captain Coo

—— Last Voyage of Captain Coo

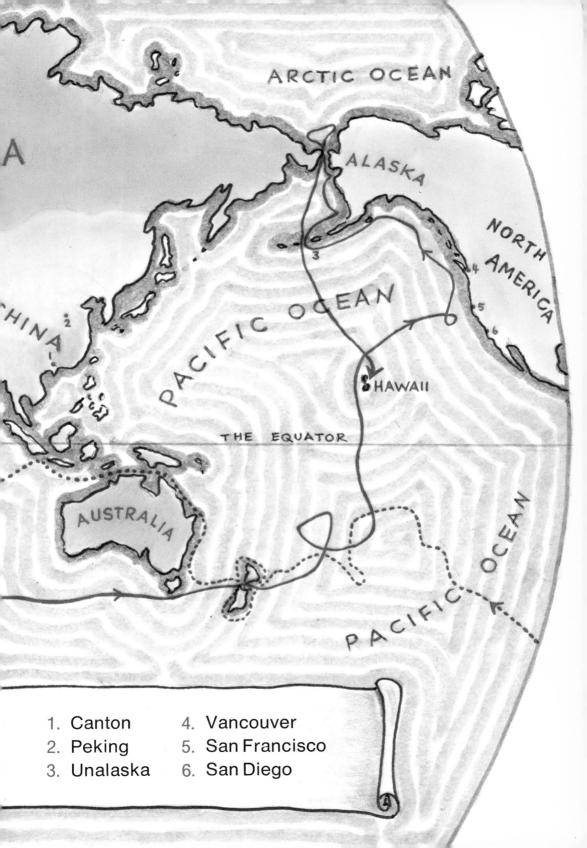

ARCTIC OCEAN

ALASKA

NORTH AMERICA

CHINA

PACIFIC OCEAN

THE EQUATOR

HAWAII

AUSTRALIA

PACIFIC OCEAN

1. Canton
2. Peking
3. Unalaska
4. Vancouver
5. San Francisco
6. San Diego

THIS IS CAPTAIN JAMES COOK, the English explorer, standing on the northeast shore of Australia. It was August, 1770. He had raised the British flag on that island

continent and was claiming it for the King of England, George III. So just before England lost her colonies in America, she gained the new colony, almost halfway around the world.

Six years later, in 1776, James Cook was sailing again from England on a voyage to the Pacific. It was July 12. The harbor of Plymouth was crowded with warships filled with British soldiers being sent to America. It would take them about one month to cross the Atlantic. The journey to Australia would take many times that long—longer, even, than it took English trading ships going out to China. There were but two ways to go—west and south around South America or southeast around Africa. If only a shorter way could be found, what a great discovery that would be!

That is exactly what James Cook was going to look for on this voyage. Taking two ships, he was to cross the Pacific to the northwest coast of America and search for a waterway that would lead from there back to the Atlantic.

He took with him two valuable charts of the far north. These had been made in 1728 by a Danish explorer, Vitus Bering, for the Czar of Russia. The Czar, whose gigantic coun-

Australia

try stretched all the way across Asia, had been curious to know if Asia and America were connected. Vitus Bering discovered that they were divided by a narrow strip of water. But on the Aleutian Islands he had heard from the Eskimos of a great land to the east which they called Aly-eska, or Alaska.

It was two full years from the time James Cook left England until he finally passed through Bering Strait into the Arctic Ocean. By this time he had practically given up hope of finding any passage through North America. He had followed the entire treacherous rocky coast north from Vancouver Island and then west along the Aleutian Islands as far as Unalaska. Although James Cook believed that what he was searching for did not exist, to be sure of it he sailed along the Arctic shore of Alaska until there were nothing to be seen ahead but a solid sheet of ice. Then he returned to the island of Unalaska, where the ships were repaired.

There the English sailors made friends with the Russian fur traders, who came in great numbers to hunt the furbearing animals. There were vast herds of seal and walrus, and thousands of otter were born each year on the Aleutian Islands. The Russians had set up furtrading posts from Alaska, which they called "New Russia," far down the American coast.

As soon as his two ships were ready, James Cook planned to go farther south for the winter. Why not go back, he thought, to the Sandwich Islands? These were lovely palm-covered islands which he had discovered on his way north across the Pacific. He had named them for his patron, Lord Sandwich. Looking through the pages of his journal, James Cook found that he had discovered those islands on January 18, 1778. It was harvest time, he remembered. Fruit and coconuts were ripe.

Alaska

Kauai

Oahu

Molokai

Maui

THE PACIFIC OCEAN

⊗ This is where
Honolulu
is today

Hawaii

EXACTLY ONE YEAR AND TWO DAYS after his first visit, James Cook's two ships, the *Resolution* and the *Discovery,* sailed into a beautiful bay on the island of Hawaii.

"Lono is here!" shouted the Hawaiians, as soon as they saw the two ships entering the harbor. Word of the captain's first visit had spread from island to island. The priests had declared that the strange white man must be Lono, God of the Harvest. Last harvest time he had appeared at Kauai Island. Now he had come to Hawaii! Thousands rushed out upon the bay to

52

greet him, their canoes heaped with fruits, coconuts, young pigs, and other gifts of the harvest.

James Cook was amazed to see so many people. They were everywhere—on the beach, in the canoes, even in the water, swimming about like fish. Very soon, in a large double canoe, came a small, withered old man, who turned out to be a priest. He climbed aboard, carrying a piece of red cloth which he respectfully draped about the shoulders of Captain Cook.

Hawaii

From then on, though he did not know it, the captain must behave like an immortal god, or he would be in danger.

One morning James Cook awoke to see the beach empty, completely deserted. When he went ashore to ask why, he was told that the beach was tabu because the great chief of the island was expected. He was returning from war against the chief of Maui. Two days later the great chief appeared in his high helmet and handsome cloak of yellow feathers.

The chief's nephew, Kamehameha, was with him. He had been with his uncle in the war. Kamehameha was later to conquer all of the warring chiefs, unite the islands into a peaceful kingdom, and in 1795 become Hawaii's first king.

Today Hawaii is one of the United States, and the statue of King Kamehameha I stands among those of other famous men in the Capitol Building in Washington, D.C.

Kamehameha was about nineteen when James Cook met him. He was a large, muscular young fellow, so strong it was said he could lift an enemy in the air on the point of his wooden spear. Everything made of iron caught his eye as he looked about the ship. He wanted his wooden spear copied in iron. Iron—that was what all the natives wanted most. They exchanged huge baskets of food for just enough iron to make a single fishhook. One boy was caught swimming under the ship, pulling out the nails. Those who came aboard picked up and carried off anything they wanted. The sailors would have seized and beaten the natives, but James Cook forbade his men ever to mistreat the natives in any way.

The Hawaiians, on the other hand, were becoming annoyed at the vast amount of food the white gods were gobbling up. They were beginning to wonder if they really were gods. One happy morning they saw the ships sail away. Nine days later they were back again. One of the masts had broken.

At night, a native stole one of the small boats. In the fight to recover it, James Cook was unable to control the sailors or the natives. As he stood on the shore motioning to the sailors not to fire the guns, he was stabbed in the back. He fell forward into the water, groaning with pain. The natives went wild. "A god does not groan!" they cried and fell upon him with their spears and killed him.

Four days later a sad procession, led by the regretful chief, came bearing a small bundle of bones, wrapped in a new red cloth, covered with sacred feathers. The sailors, who felt as if they had lost a father, lowered a small coffin into the sea, while a ten-gun salute echoed along the bay.

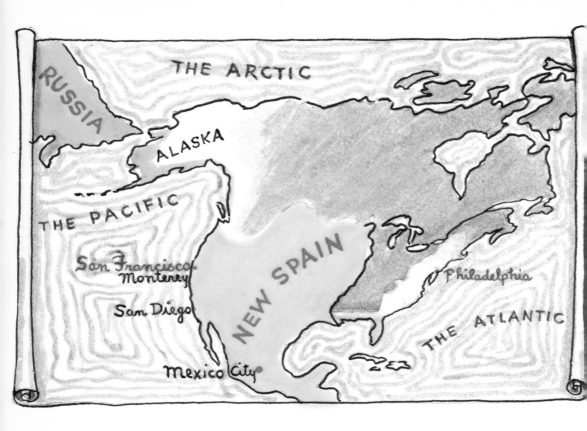

Russia
THE ARCTIC
ALASKA
THE PACIFIC
San Francisco
Monterey
San Diego
NEW SPAIN
Philadelphia
THE ATLANTIC
Mexico City

A S THIS MAP OF NORTH AMERICA SHOWS, the
Spanish claimed all of the land west of the Mississippi
River. They were decidedly disturbed to have the Russians
building their furtrading posts farther and farther down the
Pacific coast.

In 1769, the Spanish Viceroy in Mexico City, which was
the heart of "New Spain," decided to build forts along the
coast of California to protect it from the Russians. If not, the
Russians might claim all the coast as part of Alaska.

Missions for the Indians must also be built in California. A soldier named Portolá was chosen to take charge of building the forts. An elderly Franciscan monk, Fra Junípero Serra, offered to take charge of building the missions. As they were to travel overland, Portolá feared the frail monk might not have strength enough to make the difficult journey. To this Father Serra replied in his gentle manner, "I have faith that I will be given the strength. But if it be God's will that I die on the road, bury me there."

California

They were to build the first fort and mission at San Diego and one farther north at the Bay of Monterey.

"But for our Father San Francisco, is there to be no mission?" asked Fra Junípero Serra. He was told, "If Father San Francisco wishes to have a mission, let him cause his bay to be found and we will put it there."

Two ships were sent ahead with food and supplies. The travelers found them waiting in the harbor of San Diego. There, according to plan, the fort and mission were built.

On June 3, 1770, the Spanish expedition had reached the Bay of Monterey—the old monk in his dusty brown robes, the soldiers in their brown leather jackets. Father Serra began by sprinkling holy water on the land. Then he knelt by a tall cross to say the Mass. The soldiers fired their muskets and cannon. Portolá planted the Spanish flag and took possession of the land in the name of His Majesty the King of Spain.

In July, 1776, Fra Junípero Serra saw his wish come true. Overlooking the most beautiful bay on the Pacific, he began his mission dedicated to Father San Francisco. At the same time, 3,000 miles away in Philadelphia, the nation was being born to which San Francisco and all of California would one day belong.

IN 1776, THE OLDEST NATION ON THE EARTH, the great and ancient Empire of China, was over 4,000 years old. For forty years the wise Emperor Ch'ien Lung had been ruling China proudly and well, firmly believing that his empire was the one truly civilized nation under the heavens.

China

Of late the good emperor had been troubled by the number of barbarians from the west who were coming to trade. Each year more and more European traders came, bringing coarse things that the Chinese did not want and clamoring in their loud voices for the treasures of China, especially tea.

For many years Canton had been the only Chinese harbor where foreigners had been allowed to trade. Ch'ien Lung now decreed that they should not even enter the city, but must do their trading in *hongs,* or buildings, outside the city walls. The English protested, but the emperor remained firm.

Some years later ambassadors from England arrived bearing a letter to Ch'ien Lung from King George III. One morning at dawn they were told that the emperor would receive them at sunrise. It was the custom, the Chinese official explained, for visitors to kow tow to the emperor—that is, to kneel before him and bump their heads three times on the ground.

The English ambassador said, "When I approach my own king, I kneel on one knee."

Ch'ien Lung was satisfied with this sign of respect. He welcomed the English ambassadors with gifts and entertainment. It would also be his pleasure, he said, to have them remain long enough to enjoy with him the celebration of his eighty-third birthday. The English ambassadors were charméd by the emperor's invitation and felt sure that the requests which King George had made in his letter would be granted. This is part of Ch'ien Lung's answer to George III:

"You, O King, live in a distant region, far beyond the borders of many oceans. You desire humbly to share in the blessings of our civilization. Every country under Heaven and kings of all nations have sent us tribute by land and sea. We possess all things. We have no use for your products. . . . As to your request to send an ambassador to live at my Heavenly court, this cannot possibly be granted. There are many nations in Europe besides your own. If all of them asked to come to our court, how could we possibly consent?

"To you, O King, who live so far away, I have shown greater kindness than to any other nation. It is your duty, therefore, to understand my feelings and to reverently obey my instructions henceforth and for all time, so that you may enjoy the blessings of peace."

ON GEORGE WASHINGTON'S BIRTHDAY, February 22, 1784, an American ship called the *Empress of China* left New York Harbor bound for Canton. The ship arrived, and the Americans exchanged a cargo of ginseng roots for tea, porcelain, and silk.

At first the people from this newest nation on earth were called merely "New People" by the inhabitants of the world's most ancient empire. But after their new flag of Stars and Stripes had been raised above their new hong at Canton, they were known as *Hwa Chi*—"People-of-the-Flowery-Flag."

INDEX

Numbers in italics refer to maps.

Seventeen
Seventy Six
relates
the Birth of the
United States

1776

1776 ★ 1776 ★ 1776

Seventeen
Seventy Six
relates
the Birth of the
United States

1776